YOU CAN DRAW IT!

MYTHICAL BEASTS

ILLUSTRATED BY STEVE PORTER

BELLWETHER MEDIA · MINNEAPOLIS, MN

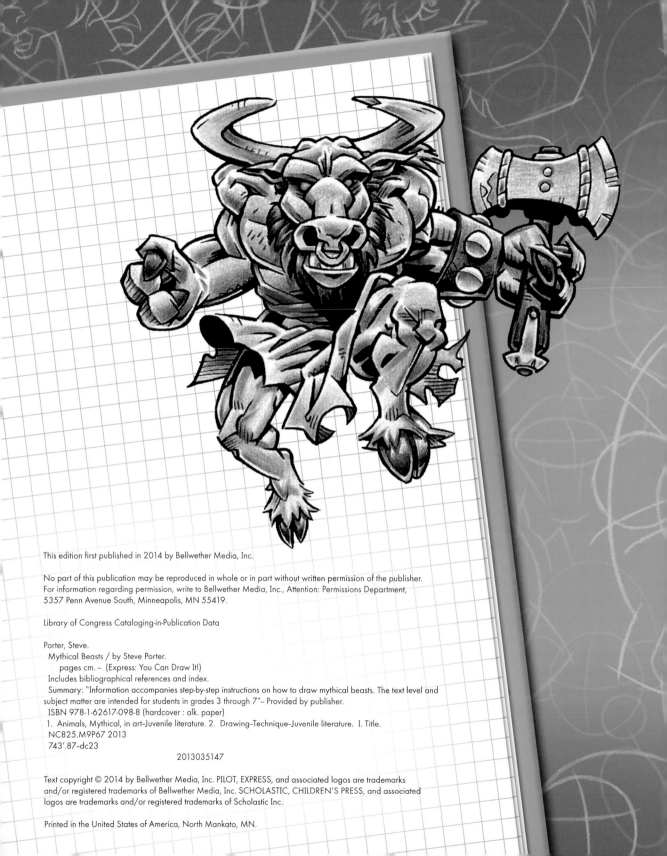

This edition first published in 2014 by Bellwether Media, Inc.

No part of this publication may be reproduced in whole or in part without written permission of the publisher.
For information regarding permission, write to Bellwether Media, Inc., Attention: Permissions Department,
5357 Penn Avenue South, Minneapolis, MN 55419.

Library of Congress Cataloging-in-Publication Data

Porter, Steve.
  Mythical Beasts / by Steve Porter.
       pages cm. – (Express: You Can Draw It!)
  Includes bibliographical references and index.
  Summary: "Information accompanies step-by-step instructions on how to draw mythical beasts. The text level and
subject matter are intended for students in grades 3 through 7"– Provided by publisher.
  ISBN 978-1-62617-098-8 (hardcover : alk. paper)
  1. Animals, Mythical, in art–Juvenile literature. 2. Drawing–Technique–Juvenile literature. I. Title.
  NC825.M9P67 2013
  743'.87–dc23
                                   2013035147

Printed in the United States of America, North Mankato, MN.

TABLE OF CONTENTS

MYTHICAL BEASTS!

Wild and fierce beasts roam the world of ancient **mythology**. Almost every culture has its own set of mythical beasts. Most of these creatures are a mix of real animals, such as horses, lizards, and birds. It is said that many of these **legendary** beasts can only be conquered by superhuman strength. Stories tell of others that may even live forever!

DRAWING FROM PHOTOS AND ILLUSTRATIONS IS A GREAT PLACE TO START. WORK YOUR WAY UP TO DRAWING FROM MEMORY OR YOUR IMAGINATION.

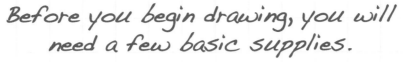

Before you begin drawing, you will need a few basic supplies.

PAPER

DRAWING
PENCILS

BLACK INK
PEN

2B OR NOT 2B?

NOT ALL DRAWING PENCILS ARE THE SAME. "B" PENCILS ARE SOFTER, MAKE DARKER MARKS, AND SMUDGE EASILY. "H" PENCILS ARE HARDER, MAKE LIGHTER MARKS, AND DON'T SMUDGE VERY MUCH AT ALL.

COLORED PENCILS
(ALL DRAWINGS IN THIS BOOK WERE FINISHED WITH COLORED PENCILS.)

ERASER

PENCIL
SHARPENER

Behemoth
The Unbeatable Brute

Behemoth is a huge ox-like beast described in the Bible. Behemoth's bones are as thick as bronze tubes. His limbs are as strong as iron rods. His tail even sways like a cedar tree! Behemoth is said to be the biggest and most powerful land creature ever to exist. Legend has it that he can only be **slain** by Leviathan at the end of the world.

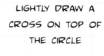

LIGHTLY DRAW A CROSS ON TOP OF THE CIRCLE

START WITH SHAPES FOR THE HEAD AND BODY

LIGHT TO DARK

BEGIN YOUR DRAWING WITH VERY LIGHT LINES. SLOWLY BUILD UP TO DARK LINES AS YOU REACH THE FINAL STEPS OF YOUR DRAWING. THIS WILL ALLOW FOR EASY CORRECTION OF MISTAKES.

ADD LINES FOR THE HORNS, LEGS, AND FACIAL FEATURES

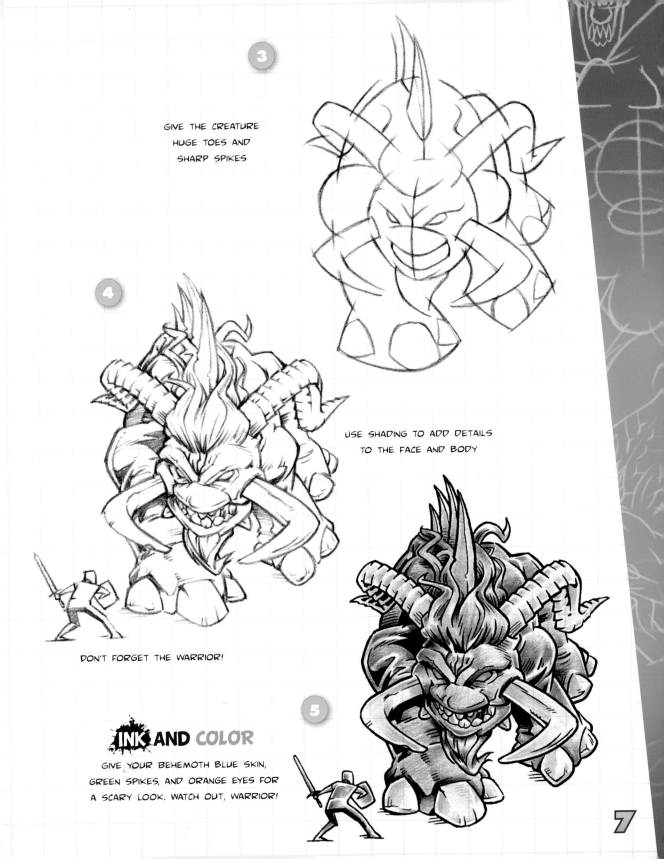

3

GIVE THE CREATURE
HUGE TOES AND
SHARP SPIKES

4

USE SHADING TO ADD DETAILS
TO THE FACE AND BODY

DON'T FORGET THE WARRIOR!

5

INK AND COLOR

GIVE YOUR BEHEMOTH BLUE SKIN,
GREEN SPIKES, AND ORANGE EYES FOR
A SCARY LOOK. WATCH OUT, WARRIOR!

Chimera

The Three-Headed Monster

The fire-breathing Chimera is a mix of three animals. She has the head of a lion. From her back rises the head of a goat. The body and head of a snake form her tail. In Greek mythology, she **terrorizes** the Turkish countryside with her strength and speed. Seeing a Chimera is bad news. It means that disasters such as storms, **volcanic** eruptions, or shipwrecks are coming!

BEGIN WITH TWO CIRCLES AND ONE OVAL FOR THE HEADS

BREAK IT DOWN

JUST ABOUT ANY SUBJECT CAN BE BROKEN INTO SMALLER PARTS. LOOK FOR CIRCLES, OVALS, SQUARES, AND OTHER BASIC SHAPES THAT CAN HELP BUILD YOUR DRAWING.

DRAW LINES FOR THE NECKS AND LEGS

ADD FEET AND SCARY
FACIAL FEATURES

3

4

PUT HAIR AND SHARP CLAWS
ON THE BEAST

5

INK AND COLOR

COLOR THE LION HEAD YELLOW
AND BROWN, THE GOAT HEAD DARK
GRAY, AND THE SNAKE HEAD LIGHT
GRAY. DON'T FORGET TO COLOR ALL
THE EYES BRIGHT RED!

Dragon
The Fire Breather

Dragons are huge, lizard-like monsters that can fly and usually breathe fire. They often have yellow eyes, **spines** on their backs, and large wings. Dragons have different meanings depending on the culture. To ancient Middle Eastern, Greek, and Roman cultures, dragons were a symbol of evil. However, the Chinese and Japanese cultures view the dragon as a symbol of wisdom.

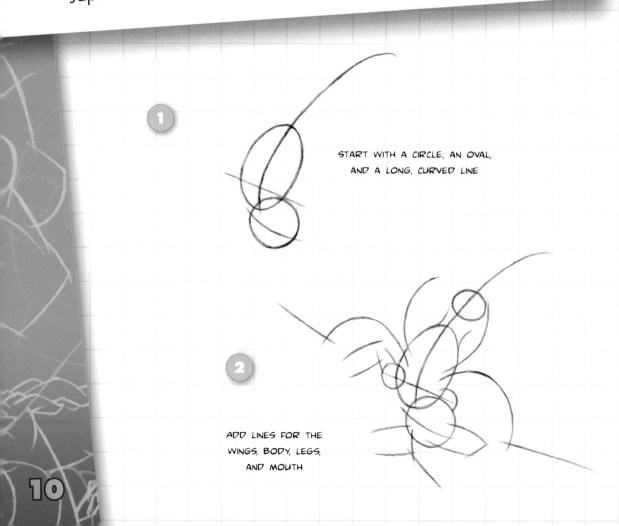

1 START WITH A CIRCLE, AN OVAL, AND A LONG, CURVED LINE

2 ADD LINES FOR THE WINGS, BODY, LEGS, AND MOUTH

3

FINISH THE WINGS, TAIL, AND LEGS

4

ADD SHARP TEETH, CLAWS, AND OTHER IMPORTANT DETAILS TO THE DRAGON

STAY BACK

HOLD YOUR PENCIL A LITTLE FARTHER BACK FROM THE TIP. THIS ALLOWS YOU TO DRAW LONGER, SMOOTHER LINES.

INK AND COLOR

PURPLE IS A GOOD COLOR FOR YOUR DRAGON. YOU MIGHT ADD SOME ORANGE TO THE BODY AND A GLOWING GREEN EYE, TOO!

5

Leviathan

The Sea Monster

Leviathan is a giant, fire-breathing sea creature in ancient Middle Eastern mythology. It is usually described as a large crocodile or sea serpent. Humans and swords are no match for Leviathan. The monster is said to **embody** the power of chaos and destruction! Only Behemoth can kill this beast at the end of the world.

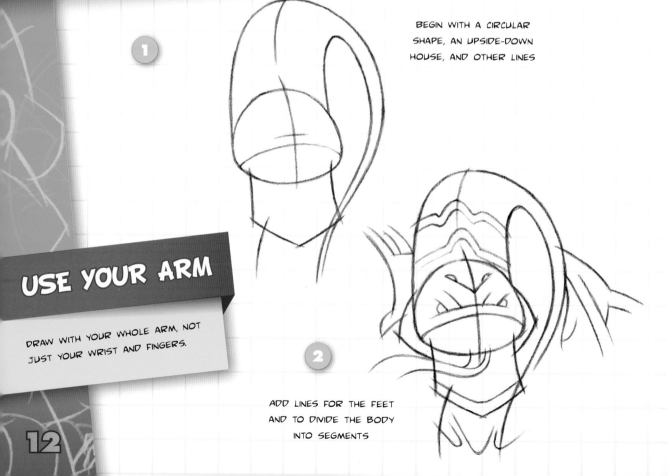

BEGIN WITH A CIRCULAR SHAPE, AN UPSIDE-DOWN HOUSE, AND OTHER LINES

USE YOUR ARM

DRAW WITH YOUR WHOLE ARM, NOT JUST YOUR WRIST AND FINGERS.

ADD LINES FOR THE FEET AND TO DIVIDE THE BODY INTO SEGMENTS

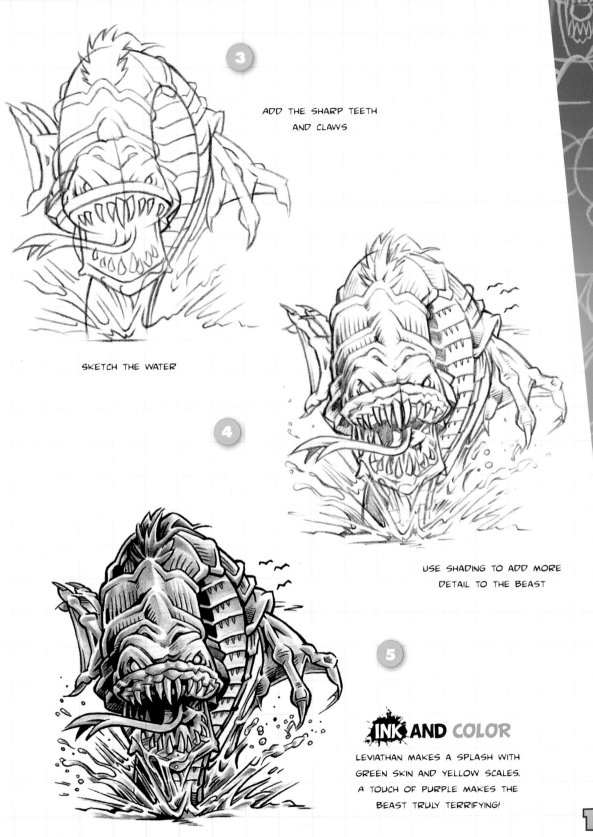

3

ADD THE SHARP TEETH
AND CLAWS

SKETCH THE WATER

4

USE SHADING TO ADD MORE
DETAIL TO THE BEAST

5

INK AND COLOR

LEVIATHAN MAKES A SPLASH WITH
GREEN SKIN AND YELLOW SCALES.
A TOUCH OF PURPLE MAKES THE
BEAST TRULY TERRIFYING!

Minotaur
The Bull-Headed Man

In Greek mythology, the Minotaur lived in a twisting **labyrinth** on the Greek island of Crete. The Minotaur was a humanlike monster with a bull's head. He survived by eating children who got lost in his labyrinth. A Greek hero named Theseus killed the Minotaur. He carried a ball of string to find his way back to the maze's entrance!

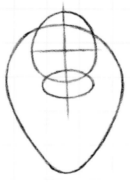

1

START WITH A CIRCLE, AN OVAL, AND A HEART-SHAPED BODY

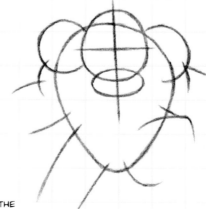

DON'T FORGET CIRCLES FOR THE SHOULDERS

2

ADD LINES FOR THE ARMS AND LEGS

ADD HORNS AND
DETAILS TO THE FACE

3

4

JUST WALK AWAY

IF YOU'RE STUCK ON A CERTAIN PART
OF YOUR DRAWING, IT IS SOMETIMES
BEST TO WALK AWAY. COME BACK LATER
WITH A FRESH APPROACH.

BE SURE TO PUT THE
WEAPON IN HIS HAND

DRAW MINOTAUR'S
HANDS AND FEET

5

INK AND COLOR

MAKE YOUR HAIRY MINOTAUR BROWN.
GIVE HIM A RED GAZE.

15

Pegasus
The Flying Stallion

Pegasus is a big, winged horse from Greek mythology. He is such a powerful flyer that he flew all the way to the heavens. There, he was given the task of carrying Zeus's thunderbolts! Because of his service to the gods, Pegasus became a **constellation** in the night sky.

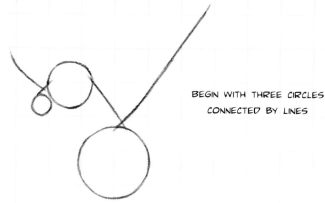

1

BEGIN WITH THREE CIRCLES
CONNECTED BY LINES

OUTLINE THE WINGS

2

ADD MORE CIRCLES AND
LINES FOR THE BODY
AND LEGS

GIVE THE HORSE
A MANE, TAIL,
AND FEATHERS

3

4

USE SHADING TO
COMPLETE THE SKETCH

FINISH THE FEATHERS
AND HOOVES

5

INK AND COLOR

PEGASUS IS WHITE, BUT USE BLUE
OR GRAY TO SHADE THE THE WINGS
AND BODY. BLACK OUTLINES WILL
HELP THE HORSE FLY OFF THE PAGE!

17

Phoenix
The Firebird

The phoenix is a large bird that has bright red and gold feathers that are said to **emit** sunlight. This blazing wingspan is impressive, but a phoenix's life span is even more so. It lives for more than 500 years at a time! At the end of its life, a phoenix builds a nest, stands in it, and lights it on fire. As the fire burns, a new phoenix flies up from the ashes! The phoenix is a symbol of **immortality** to the ancient Greek, Roman, and Egyptian cultures.

1 START WITH A SMALL CIRCLE ABOVE AN OVAL

SEE THE BIG PICTURE

WAIT TO ADD DETAILS UNTIL YOU ARE HAPPY WITH THE BASIC SHAPE OF YOUR DRAWING. YOU DON'T WANT TO SPEND TIME DETAILING A PART OF YOUR DRAWING THAT WILL BE ERASED LATER.

2 LIGHTLY OUTLINE THE WINGS AND TAIL

3

ADD FEATHER
DETAILS TO
THE BIRD

4

MAKE THE FEATHERS
LOOK LIKE FLAMES

5

INK AND COLOR

SET YOUR PHOENIX ON FIRE
WITH BRIGHT RED, ORANGE, AND
YELLOW FEATHERS.

19

Troll
The Giant Forest Dweller

People who wander the forests of **Scandinavia** should watch for trolls. They are said to lurk between the trees! Although they are not very smart, trolls are big, strong, and like to eat people. They are most active at night. If they leave their caves during the day, the sunlight turns them into stone!

DRAW A CIRCLE INSIDE
AN OVAL

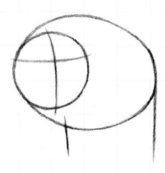

LIGHTLY DRAW A
CROSS ON TOP OF
THE CIRCLE

DRAW THE EYES
AND NOSE

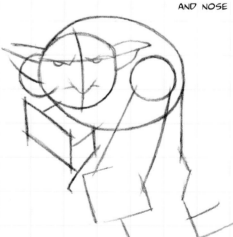

ADD SHAPES FOR
THE ARMS, LEGS,
AND EARS

ADD FINGERS, TOES, AND THE TAIL

ADD IMPORTANT
DETAILS WITH
LITTLE LINES
AND SHADING

DON'T FORGET THE
TROLL'S HAMMER!

MIX AND MATCH

YOU CAN MIX COLORS BY GOING
OVER A PREVIOUSLY COLORED
SECTION WITH A NEW COLOR.

INK AND COLOR

TURN YOUR TROLL INTO STONE
WITH NATURAL COLORS. USE
BROWN TO SHOW THAT HIS
HAMMER IS MADE OF WOOD.

21

GLOSSARY

constellation—a pattern of stars in the night sky

embody—to represent in physical form

emit—to give off

immortality—being able to live forever

labyrinth—a maze of winding passageways

legendary—related to legends; a legend is a well-known tale that has been around for a long time.

mythology—the set of stories or beliefs of a culture

Scandinavia—an area of northern Europe; the Scandinavian countries are Denmark, Norway, and Sweden.

slain—killed in battle

spines—sharp, pointed parts that project out from an animal

terrorizes—scares someone

volcanic—relating to volcanoes; a volcano is a hole in the earth that releases hot, melted rock.

TO LEARN MORE

At the Library

Berry, Bob. *How to Draw Magical, Monstrous & Mythological Creatures*. Irvine, Calif.: Walter Foster Publishing, 2012.

Children's Book of Mythical Beasts & Magical Monsters. New York, N.Y.: DK Publishing, 2011.

Drake, Ernest. *Dr. Ernest Drake's Monsterology: The Complete Book of Monstrous Beasts*. Cambridge, Mass.: Candlewick Press, 2008.

On the Web

Learning more about mythical beasts is as easy as 1, 2, 3.

1. Go to www.factsurfer.com.

2. Enter "mythical beasts" into the search box.

3. Click the "Surf" button and you will see a list of related Web sites.

With factsurfer.com, finding more information is just a click away.

INDEX